Angel of the Dawn

....

poems

Marlaina Donato

Ekstasis Multimedia
Blairstown, New Jersey

Angel of the Dawn/Marlaina Donato
Blairstown, New Jersey: Ekstasis Multimedia, LLC, 2014
Ekstasis Multimedia: www.booksandbrush.net

ISBN-13: 978-0615799414
ISBN-10: 0615799418

Photography and design: Marlaina Donato

...For the angel with the shining sickle who severs the flower, and in its grave, sows the seed of another more brilliant than any before it...

Contents

Translating Ecstasy

Synapse

Go

Where God's lute

Wafts through the corridors of a deaf
world.

Go

Where discontent

Empties into oceans dissolving regret.

Go

Where Beauty is born

From a single thought

Stretched across imperfections.

Birth

Life is a series of deaths...

Every hour, something stops breathing-

A dream

A fire

A belief;

A heart stops beating.

The final death-

Feared

Prolonged

Mourned;

The final closing of the book,

Rarely seen as the birth

That ends all deaths.

Angel of the Dawn

Just beneath the surface of sleep,

Your smile tastes like sunlight,

And Your soul is full of morning.

Come to me, Angel of the Hours,

Into the temple of my heart

That holds the altar of Your beauty,

The book of Your eyes.

Beneath the surface of waking,

Before this life,

I gave You the key to my nights.

Open me, Angel of the Dawn;

Open me.

Heart's Turning

Wind washes the morning clean,

Baptizing a soul battered by dreams

And faces sleep never forgets.

In the cascading wind,

One remaining leaf

Leaves the branch.

A dream lets go.

Promise

The soil is prepared...

Winter-numb earth

Upturns into a fertile womb

By the pain of the plough.

Does the field,

Stripped

And

Burned,

Know of the bounty to come?

Orpheus

Bow to string

Hand to instrument

Once a tree in a wind-swept forest

Now reincarnated into symphony

Flesh upon wood

Hypnotic alchemy

Each giving the other a soul

Translating ecstasy

Hour of Flight

Follow the path of shadow

Where memories lean into the water;

Do not be afraid to touch the river

And its dark lips whispering night.

The truth is- we die many times

Before we are born again.

Take the morning's smile

Strewn across the heavens...

Play with it; take its freedom.

The dying is over.

Trust the bright coins of dawn

And buy an hour of flight.

A Million Selves

A flower has been ripped from the root,

A flower that will not bloom again;

But you do not know

An eternal garden lives in me...

A garden so vast, so infinite,

Heaven is but a shadow in its hand.

A self has been shattered,

A self I will never again be;

But you do not know

A million selves live in me-

In my Soul that is greater than birth,

Wiser than death,

Stronger than *this,*

Your fist

Your greed.

I will not bleed

Your memory.

Joy

Joy lives in the river of tears;

A nymph enclosed in the water's depth,

She tends the fires of forgotten smiles.

Her throat is pearled with memories,

And her voice sweetens

The river's bitter miles.

Holding the warmth of the coldest rapid

And a lantern for the darkest wave,

She leaps over rock and pitfall,

Harnessing the rainbow,

Adorning the soul's empty cave.

When tears flood the banks,

Clear are her prism eyes.

From the mud of despair,

Her torchlight gleams,

And thrown a coin of faith,

She will rise.

Creature Kin

I am the serpent.

See the world through my eyes

And wear a hood of wisdom

When you walk through the underground

Of human nature.

I am the eagle.

Borrow my wings

And drink the sunlight

When you aim for uncharted skies

Of potential.

I am the cheetah.

Run with me

And brush the shoulders of the wind

To temper your power

With moral grace.

I am the snow leopard.

Seek my summit bed

When your mind is drained

Of answers

And the inner sage will awaken.

I am the owl.

Know your nocturnal path

And forgive and see beyond

Your illusionary darkness.

I am the butterfly.

Remember my modesty

And the ability to drink the moment.

I am the chameleon.

Remember my secret

Of survival

And my instinct to wear experience

Like a shield.

I am the ant.

Remember my determination

And willingness to work

With others with focus and humility.

I am the loon.

Remember my song in the night

And the medicine of solitude.

I am the lame gull.

Remember my persecution.

Dark Sustenance

Autonomy

Tiny spider sleeping

Magnificent web netting a sunbeam

Tiny spider sleeping

In a home she built from a thread

Who thought

You could accomplish such magnitude

Such symmetry

From your own being

And so too the soul

If only we remember

Ostara

Leaf, blade and blossom

Bear the scars of snow.

Earth giving birth

To green.

Mother Eternal,

You offer your breasts of rain.

Tree, flower, and grain

Bear the memory of snow.

Earth giving birth

To herself,

Mother Eternal.

Vesta

Chosen by birth and initiated by fire,

She has tended the altar;

Year upon year, night upon night,

She has introduced incense to flame

And offered the first fruits of her soul.

A lifetime of rehearsal so easily dissolved

In the poverty of preparation

When the god, at last, arrives...

Can a life ever be ready for the glance

From immortal eyes?

Can a heart not quake

Beneath its own desire?

Can a cup not shatter

From its own fullness?

Journey Back to Innocence

My feet reach terrain never crossed

And rocks unforeseen

In search of innocence lost.

Heaven and Hell, a heart drifts

In between.

I am a stranger here

With no map in hand

Or shoes to conquer the stone;

Yet I know this foreign land-

The soul, the flesh, and the bone.

Long, I have been a child out in the night

With a canteen of dreams

The darkness spilled.

But here, the stars are bright

And my wings cannot be stilled!

My steps are bloody,

Yet they defy the thorn,

And wisdom warns to turn away.

Heaven or Hell, a heart is torn.

Which must I obey?

Thirst weakens will,

And the wind persuades thought.

A clear pool beckons in the mist.

Against this cage, my fear has fought.

I duel with tear and fist.

I weep and wade in the water's quiet eyes.

Though, I have bathed in the mighty sea,

Here, I am baptized,

And my lost reflection embraces me.

I am That I am

We are living flame,

Hearts born of fire,

Souls sired by the stars.

The only ones of our kind-

And the last.

Irretrievable

Day's jewel shatters in the west.

Night plummets between

The sharp edges of birdsong.

April continues to bloom-

Inspiration or habit, only she knows.

While the spirit, a broken lute,

Remembers a song

It will never sing again.

Legacy

Pages yellowed by time,

Words etched in ember.

Stark in their light,

Glowing but leaning toward death;

Her signature- a pirouette of ink,

Right-hand corner.

Her spirit long-flown,

Her name unremembered,

No longer the name of my mother

But a woman who spun words

From blood-stained silk.

A woman, a glorious sun

Burning in verse,

A forgotten poet singing

To her daughter

Who holds her words like bread

In a time of long famine.

Bread of dark sustenance, of grain

That says, "I, too, hungered."

Bread for these dark nights

And dawns with no answers.

Second Birth

How fragile, how frightening

This hour...

Silent flower

Lifting her face after the storm.

Life hollowed by pain

Now empty to contain

Only this beauty.

How fragile, how frightening

This absence of rage...

A flower opening her eyes after frost;

After devastation, nothing lost.

Youth, love and grace regained.

With wisdom, all attained.

First birth- learn to walk, to cry.

Second birth- learn, earn to fly.

One of Ten-Thousand Names

Goddess spoke to me

In the voice of the wind,

And I learned a different song.

Goddess gazed at me

Through the eyes of the moon,

And I became beautiful.

Goddess touched me

With hands of twilight rain,

And I was healed.

Goddess found me

On the battlefield of broken dreams

And held me in Her arms of peace.

Sanctuary

Muse, you have been here;

Here in the fragile dawns,

In the morning deer,

In alabaster snows,

In the birch against the blue...

I will remember you

In this room,

In the sun's gold goodbye

Through cold glass,

In the ecstatic lapse

Of time

Between scars,

In the oak leaf's falling

And in the answers

Of the stars.

Night Waters

Ascension

Blinding darkness

Our souls spilling backward

Catching a wave of fire

Extinguishing into

Pulse

Heartbeat

Sun

Lovers into Beloved

Awake! Cocoon of flesh forgotten

Hearts, the weight of a dream

On the breath of Now

Chrysalis Outgrown

Lightning scars the ashen cheek of sky;

Silver light bleeds into the blowing cloths

Of the wind.

Barefoot on parched grass,

I cast off my soiled scarf of dreams.

I undress my life

And stand naked before the storm.

Hair once bound now tangled

By the thunder's furious hands.

Heaven's pewter cup brims,

Quenching thirst of grass and skin.

I laugh at the umbrella once clung-to

As my breasts drink the rain,

And into the storm's vehement embrace,

Cast all of myself.

Requiem for a Star

In the night's voiceless cathedral,

Legions of stars burn steadily,

A distant dais of prayer candles.

Somewhere, the birth of a new star,

A newly-lit wick,

Is celebrated while another dies,

Beaming its light without encore

Or ovation,

Bequeathing eons of prayers,

Generations of wishes

To the unheeding darkness.

In a crowded night,

Who notices the candle gone out?

Disciple

God of my soul, prophet of my pain,

You arrived like the dawn,

Bearded and bronzed in the gleam

Of the corridor's end.

With eyes that harbor heaven,

You hold my life like a dove

In Your sun-clenched hand.

Into love's tentative sea,

I cast faith's gold-woven nets

Of constancy

And gather wisdom,

Harvesting until the nets break.

And my heart, walking on water,

Shimmers and dances like diamonds.

Soul-Quest

Famished, searching for sustenance,

The soul seeks another soul,

But its image remains unfound,

A heart beating among strangers.

The Fish

He glides through night waters,

Outwitting a maze of shadows and lilies.

While the others grapple over morsels,

He wonders what the moonlight is-

Silver rain, ring-less and mute?

Lilies of light floating like stars

On a watery tapestry?

Surely, the moonbeams

Are the boat lights of angels...

No, they are celestial arrows

That wound with longing for answers

Or wings.

In an Old Church

Morning scatters a galaxy of snow

Over black-limbed maples

In soldier's stance.

We walk through the meadow

Once haunted with June butterflies

And breeze into the old church

On the corner.

Wind presses its cold cheek

Against the windows,

Eavesdropping on a century of prayers.

Nearly a year's soil beneath our footfalls,

Seeming a lifetime amid

The blowing stars of snow,

Amid the white-winged ghosts

Of butterflies.

Familiar

Cat purring to my heartbeat

Moment of perfect understanding

Words superfluous

No explanation why I read poetry

And never read directions

Or why I wear moccasins in winter

No explanation of her taste in mice

Or what she dreams of in the sun

Kindred spirits

Madrigal

Sapphire hour

Closing doors of the day

Silent walking

Pause

Listen

A madrigal in the twilight

Wind chimes blowing

From a house somewhere

In the blue

Citadel

Stripped even of myself,

You are all I own-

Womb of my birth,

Beauty of this earth.

In your arms I have survived.

In your arms I will die.

There is an army coming to plunder,

Coming to rape.

I am without sword, without escape,

But I have my fist

And the key, the Me

They will never find.

Sanctum never to splinter or fall;

Stake, break, take all-

Never to surrender, only remember

This Faith, this Fire, this Infinity...

Sanctuary, sanctuary;

Between yesterday's blown-out flame

And tomorrow's unseen face,

Beloved or burning sky,

You are safety's last embrace.

Beloved or burning sky,

My pain is polished

In the gold fury of your fire,

And my soul will forever rise

From your desire,

Phoenix eternal.

You are all I ever owned...

Womb of my birth,

Beauty of this earth.

Prism Garden

Magnolias After the Rain

I exalt Life-

The gross matter which encumbers me.

So, Death do I pardon

For hesitating to answer my request.

The rain is sweet on the bough,

And I am here to witness

Spring's timeless glory.

At the Crossroads

I came to the crossroads of Self

Where an old woman spun white threads

And moonbeams ran down their lengths

Like spring spiders.

I offered the Fate who determined

The length of life

Sweet wine of praise,

But she continued to spin,

Moonlight spilling off her wheel like

Water.

I danced for her and gathered fruit

Of faith and sentiment

In exchange for a thread

That could wrap around the earth twice.

Tired and bewildered by her silence,

I stepped closer

And saw that she had my eyes.

Her hair blew in the midnight wind

And shimmered like moonshine

On the willow that dwells

By the river.

I stepped closer

And saw that the smiling, weathered face

Was mine.

Magdalene

Out of the tomb,

Out of three day's eclipse of the soul,

You rise, enshrouded

In the shining garments of the morn.

From the Void, you fly back to me.

...Rabboni, Rabboni...

I reach to touch the life

I may no longer touch.

You have risen only to entomb me

With longing.

...Rabboni, Rabboni...

After you ascend, my hands

May then touch your feet,

But when you return to me,

Your spirit will be aqua glass

Blown by the heavens.

Near your beauty and fragility

That will no longer bear

The weight of my love,

I will bow to your divinity

But mourn the man

Whose sandal remains

Imprinted in the dust

Of one woman's heart.

Daughter of the Phoenix

Fire will forge my death

And fire will forge my birth.

I stand beneath the sun,

My destiny foreknown.

In ash I will die;

From ash I will ascend.

As my mother and her mother,

I am a child of the phoenix,

Daughter of the flame's auriferous hell.

With the few who overstep

Death's precipice,

I hold fast to the cocoon;

In Death's womb,

Consecrated by the soul's black fire,

I wait.

I bear the night's anguished wound,

For I know

As all children of the phoenix know,

This is not my first death

Nor will it be my last.

From fire I came;

From fire I will go.

With each descent I will ascend

From my bed of ashes

Toward a triumphant heaven

With wings,

With wings,

With wings.

Visitation

In the barren desert of our days,

You may pass a prism garden

Lush with the light of a quiet soul

And you will know she has been there.

In the dark yearning of our years,

You may find a bountiful table

Overflowing with the abundance

Of an honest heart,

And you will know she has been there.

In the thorned dance to our destinations,

You may hear the haunting music

Of a bird,

And breathless, you will pause to listen,

And you will know she has been there,

An angel among us.

Blue Infinity

I do not know

If I am dancing this dream

Or dreaming the dance.

Days are flowers

Trembling against joy's illumined breast;

Nights, the silver wings of angels

Ascending into the storm's

Breathless fury.

Every step spins my soul

Into blue infinity.

As long as we have dreamt of Love,

Love has dreamt of us.

Spared

A weeping loon

Sends her prayer upon the waves

And listens for her echo to return

Upon the hour's dark wind.

It is the only thing that returns,

The only portion of her soul

Time or thief has not yet taken-

Her song in the starless nights.

Dark Night of the Soul

We search to find the phoenix,

A single feather from its burning flight,

Proof there is something of ourselves

Left to burn, to give light.

Dreams that remain are crimson leaves;

Two, three, no more, cling to November.

Our own lives, like trees in the twilight,

Though, entranced by forgetfulness,

Must put forth a solitary branch,

A single,

Faithful twig

That hopes for spring,

Hopes for all the others

Slumbering in darkness

On nights like this.

Provenance

Leaves pressed into a book

Mark a forgotten day,

Significance lost in a torrent of years.

Now impervious to season, far from limb,

Do they remember

The busy metropolis of roots

Or the galaxy of spring buds...

Can they recite the mute history of bark?

Do they remember their sire,

The towering bard

Who put words to the wind...

Do their souls return as birds,

Spilling harmony into the dawn?

Hotel Lobby

One hundred people

Pushing

Waiting

Passing

Shoulder-to-shoulder isolation

Each his own continent

With no connecting flights

Flames of the Stars

Metamorphosis

I have seen the flames of the stars

Flicker in the wind.

Like them, I embraced the night

When day threw her stones.

...And I have walked with Magdalene.

I have stood on foggy shores

With rebellion in the whitened waves

And in my hands.

I denied shelter when my nets

came up empty.

...And I have walked with Simon.

I have doubted

The most brilliant of miracles

And mocked the visions of other men.

...And I have walked with Thomas.

I have been tempted by gold and the

Silver of the earth.

I have betrayed and writhed in despair.

...I have walked with Judas.

Master Key

There are no lifetimes of happiness,

Only moments.

There are no destinations,

Only resting places.

There are no changes,

Only seasons.

Bridegroom

When the door between worlds

Is left ajar,

You come to me in the night

And burn above me

With shining wings

Of infinity

And a whisper inaudible

To the irreverent day.

Night Angel,

Lover of the storm's beating heart,

Husband of the Heavens,

Bridegroom of my soul,

I have forsaken lifetimes of constancy

For one elusive touch

That is no longer mine at dawn's coming.

Let me brave the thunder

Beneath your wings,

Beloved, eclipse the sun once more,

Once more.

The Bather

He swims in a platinum river,

Enveloped by the tides.

Are you man or god,

Strong as the stones

At the river's heart,

Soft and shimmering as rain,

Gold and alabaster

Carved by the silver fingers of the waters?

From this bluff, I cannot see your eyes,

Yet I know they are deep

And the color of the river's thoughts

And rapids are not half as wild

As your soul.

...Dancing, dissolving...

Tonight, in dreams, I will be silver water.

Eurydice

What is left to startle my soul

Now that I have tasted you?

What beauty, what burning,

What exquisite pain

Could ever suffice again?

In the deaf storm of my life,

Orpheus, I have heard your song;

Now I can live.

Into the deep sleep of hell,

You have followed my desire

To lead me from the abyss...

I know how the myth ended before,

Before I tasted you.

Please, this time, do not turn.

Do not turn to look behind.

Leave doubt in the depths.

Let me taste the sunlight.

Elegy for a Self

Her heart was a cup of sky;

One sip and you could taste

The storm over the mountains.

Her hand was a chisel

Against the defiant marble of dreams,

And her soul, a gossamer morning

Flung over the night.

She did not know the fragility

Of the goblet

Or the ravenous thirst;

The cold reality within the stone

Or the sword within the darkness.

Close her eyes;

Let the twilight take her.

Let her sisters sing the moon

Over her memory.

Cover her with disheveled night

And the leaves that blow

In the face of the storm.

Let fire bury fire.

Heather

Across the heather-embroidered moor,

A spirit walks...

Be cautious, my child,

When you hear her skirts

Billowing in the wind.

Some say she is a fay

Who weeps beneath the moon.

Others say she is a poet

Who has come back with unbraided hair

To find verses she has left behind.

Signature

Listening to the haiku

Of whispering waters,

Weeping pine boughs lean

To drink from reflection.

The pewter-wash of the lake's expanse

Fades into mist, into memory,

And the dreamer, tracing the shore,

Searches for the artist's lost signature.

Soul's Remembrance

The snow-tired heart

Awakens to spring,

And the night offers incense

Of thawing earth and April rain.

It is then

The soul will hear the litany of the winds

And look above its own greatness

To the stars and know which ones

Are the lanterns of the gods.

Resurrection

Cocooned in the dawn's gilded shroud,

I cast my heart's tattered remnant

Into the unknown.

A morning moon gathers her silver net

From an ebbing sea

While straight and unfaltering

As an arrow, I leave

The impoverished safety of the bow;

Unconquered in triumph's ascent,

I soar into the eagle's ecstasy...

All around me, scattering, falling,

The golden dust of outgrown dreams,

Yellow roses thrown

From the hands of the rising sun.

Sun on Water

Love Song to India

Once, I looked into the dark fire

Of your eyes

And danced in your perfumed temples

Garlanded with flowers

To your painted gods of gold.

From a dais of silk,

I kissed your impoverished hands

And envied the faceless grace

Of an untouchable

Walking your streets of dust.

I drank until intoxication

On your quest for beauty

And worshipped until nirvana

The raga of your broken soul.

I tasted your kiss in your cardamom

And inhaled eternity

From your sandalwood pyre.

I saw your mother's smile

Mirrored in the Ganges.

Once, I lived and died

In your ancient arms;

Though, transformed and veiled by time,

I have never forgotten you,

Barefoot, bejeweled, dark-eyed India.

Castaway

Outside, new moon dissolved by rain

Inside, these four walls

Island, no way off

Infinity of days

Waiting for this fire to be seen

Hope long dead

Dead as the last grains of incense

Burned hours ago

Sweetness barely lingering

In bitter memory

Escape

I waded through the meadow's

Wind-braided hair,

Scented grass to my knee,

And climbed the summit

And mocked the distant

Earthbound silhouettes

Against the billowing blue cape

Of twilight.

Great waves of wind

Bathed the wounds of the soul

Until it was no longer I

Who stood on the hill's patina brow

But a shining seraph

Catching the first star's silver

On my wings.

And far away...

Mingling with the muffled voices

Of approaching night,

The soft, crackling gallop

Of a mare through dry grass,

And on her wind-saddled back,

A girl singing toward home.

Biography in Driftwood

In a season of fury,

A storm ripped out a tree's soft heart

And set it adrift

Upon a ceaseless world of water.

Driftwood, hewn by

Fingers of circumstance

And seasoned against hearts of stone

Until you were impervious

To the rage of nights.

Burnished, sea-gray veteran,

How long the journey

To this vast, virgin shore;

Infinite hours proceeding toward

God

Beloved

Self

Finding all of them,

None of them.

Elusive trinity, ever present, ever unseen

In the transience of the tides,

The constancy of the swells.

Driftwood, refugee of the storm

Lost child of the forest,

Half-hewn creature of the sea...

Soft heart made wise and beautiful

In the harsh, exquisite womb

Of the waters.

A survivor of remembrance, this wood,

Polished and all too human;

A life like mine

That lends its voice to the Inaudible.

What we are, the wave has made.

Prayer by Prayer

Days die on the bough,

Untasted, uneaten, longed-for

With a hunger that rages.

(When did the mornings
Lose their sacredness?)

Age of the soul, not the body,

Tarnishes sunlight like forgotten silver.

A thief without a face

Pulled youth up like a weed

And crushed her temples

Prayer by prayer into silence.

(When did the mornings
Lose their sacredness?)

For Spring to Come...

Autumn...

And the forest has drunk its cup of time

Only to drink again from Rebirth.

Roots...

Limbs...

Drifting leaves...

Oh, rain-wept tree,

Unclothed ladder of the seasons,

Sleep.

Dream.

For spring to come,

Death must come first.

With the Wind's Turning

I thought I saw you,

Barely touched by the years.

Three steps behind you,

In the deafening crowd,

I thought I saw you.

The heart lives many lives then forgets.

Would you have known me

Beneath this painted mask of time?

Would your heart have remembered,

If only for a second,

Like a jewel of sun on water

That glimmers and glints

And then is gone

With the wind's turning?

Dusk

Sleep, dreaming of the dead

Dusk, threshold of storm

Leaves flying in ghost-wind

Ashes, embers drifting

The living, the dead-

Neither are free

Embers burning me

With wisdom

Dream of my father

Wearing his plaid shirt

Sitting at the table, weeping

Sleeping

Caught between worlds

Crying for the dead

And the dead crying for the living

Chasm

Chasm between ecstasy

And the sobriety of reason

Pause between the spaces of Now

When the music ceases

And the flaws of the dancer are seen

When hunger learns the difference

Between the crumbs and the feast

And the value of the least

Can no longer satiate

Pray to bear the pauses

And their weight

All Saint's Day

October's end

Fire of leaves smoldering

In the ash of cold rain

Dark water holding the memory of light

At a restless hour when all things

Murmur the reluctance of change

First Breath

Who I am

For you who never asked who I am

I am a blade turned on itself

Too unwilling to draw blood

For you who never asked who I am

I have a name

And a heart wasted in vain

I gave a soul

And a thousand selves

To mend you whole

For you who never asked who I am

I have a voice

In this silent war

I am not your whore

Or your stepping stone

For you who never asked who I am

I am a storm you cannot see

Gathering wind

Gathering speed

For you who never asked who I am

I am a force

You will reckon with

A source

You underestimated

Desecrated

Dismissed with careless hand

To answer what you never asked

This is who I am

Ashore

Night folds a velvet wing

Over darkening waters.

Compliant waves, undeterred by rock,

Swirl into sleep.

A life spared from the deep

Rests on the shore,

Waiting for slumber too still for dreams.

Emergence

Night of metamorphosis

Out of the chrysalis

Eons of winter obliterated

Out of the abyss

Out of the cocoon toward noon

Into light

And bright beauty

Wings tired from birth

Wings not of this earth

Initiate

Through the underworld of self

He travels the night shore,

Aware of the black wave

Cresting in silence.

Remembering the succulent kiss of sun,

He glances backward once more

Then turns to face

The nocturnal teacher.

Persephone

Your smile is carved from sunlight

As you happen to pass through my

Darkness.

You are a butterfly streaming light,

Yet you brave my heart's net of shadows.

Before you depart on the wind,

Teach me about transience,

Speak of wings;

Remind me

I, too, am a child of the cocoon.

First Breath

I left my crutch of pain

At the water's edge;

I unfurled my wings

In the blind, summer dusk,

And my veil of sleep blew away...

I emptied my cup of tears

In Love's great expanse

And drank laughter's wine.

The faiths I had lost

Washed in with the night.

I cleaned the stains from childhood's lace

And mended the tatters of broken smiles.

I opened the door to my inner quiet,

And my splintered selves came home.

Tonight,

I hold the unfaltering flame of Self,

And as the sea leaves

Bracelets of foam around my ankles,

I take my first breath of Now.

Parole

Out of darkness

Into chaos of sun and sound

Dress, speak, continue on

Scared for eye to meet eye

Scared the world can see this soul

Still soiled from hell

Dress, speak, continue on

As if these shoulders

Never carried the burden of self

Yes, I have murdered

I have stolen

I have shattered

My own dreams

My own potential

My own innocence

Dress, speak, continue on

Terrified to trust

This scarred freedom

Haiku

September undresses the myrtle;

Fuchsia river of blossoms

And fierce tears.

Beneath a painted umbrella,

I walk, invisible

Against the day's gray heart,

Footsteps reciting the poetry

Of torn flowers.

Plenty

Spring tree just reborn

Reaching into heaven with full hands

Gestation of snow, womb of buds

Peridot hour of jeweled innocence

Solitary reveler walking on shadows

Spring heart reborn

Reaching into heaven with full hands

Envy

Purple crocus, already dead

Beneath March snow.

A hopeful friend,

She smiled for only a day or two

And promised to return next year.

The birds are home again,

And their song closes the day.

Happy singers, the sky is threatening

Yet still you sing...

From a Distant Window

Spell

Wisteria moon intoxicated with light

Night, drunk on awakening

May, eager and undaunted

As the epiphany of a smile

That leaves the heart stunned

Love in solitary dance

In dervish-spin

Ecstasy as futile

As a snowflake in the sun

Blossomed youth, an honored guest

Sups on unattainable dreams

Too beautiful to die in vain

Too soon sober

The world will return to itself

Reason disoriented as a moth in daylight

1967

Sunlight shines through a memory;

A dancing child with summer in her hair

When the air smelled like rain and youth

And the world raged beyond

The perimeter of our dreams.

Sunlight shines through a memory;

An artist on the street

With blue eyes like a sleeping sea

And my skirt that made you think

Of Gypsies...

We danced and drank the hour.

We knew we were only leaves,

Thoughts lost on the winds,

Memories shining through the sunlight

Of a distant day.

Centuries

Indigo tapestry of sky

Embroidered with stars

Centuries of burning

Canopied over our insignificance

Eyes heavenward

Infinite hunger for the Unattainable

The Star

With a net to catch the stars,

I ran through the night.

A daughter of the earth,

I reached far beyond my gaze

To a star holding the west with quiet light

And dreams of my childhood days.

Through starry fields,

I roamed without roots, without wings,

And you dared to shine

Greater than the moon.

You left your trusted throne,

Night's ancient king,

And followed me to youth's blazing noon.

But I peered into my net

When the journey was done

And found only dried leaves of despair.

Beyond my ladder of hope

And your stairway of time,

I was here…and you still there,

Despite my heart's undaunted climb.

Passages

The moon is a bronze flower

Wilting and waning in the east.

Suspended in silence

Between night and dawn.

Unseduced by sleep, I, too,

Am suspended in the night...

Somewhere

Between birth's maternal breast

And death's inevitable embrace.

An old dream limps in the wind

And settles in a temporary doorway

Of hope.

As a homeless man,

Hungry, forgotten.

My eyes remain sober

As my kin, my lover, and my friend

Sleep somewhere

Beneath the night's star-stitched blanket.

But for me, there is no bed prepared.

Destiny has eluded me.

I consult the Sybil, the old gypsy moon

And her near-death eyes.

There are no perpetual dwellings,

Only doorways...

We are only guests

Beneath her withered smile.

Dawn, like a red-haired woman,

Arches her body across the east,

Her womb a passage for the sun

And sleep for tired eyes.

Letter to the Soul

You have found no reflection

In the waters,

No mirror in man...

Yet, you have been

A flower's sweet song of fragrance

And circles of rain

In a storm-blackened pond.

You have conquered

The swift current of years,

Impervious to the transgressions of time.

Who am I to question the path

You have hewn for me?

I am but another costume

You have chosen

For Destiny's masquerade,

A needy child,

An embryo of experience

Beside your ancient divinity.

In the hollow heart of nights,

I have seen a flicker of fire

Through this maze of pain...

Has it been you, listening

From a distant window,

Though, my darkness has tried

To burn the beauty from your existence?

How many times I have abandoned you

By the bitter wayside

Only to find that you've gently

Limped your way home once again...

How many times I have mistaken

A demon's eyes for your shelter...

How many times I have forsaken you,

Soul of mine,

Soul Divine?

I am stripped of rebellion,

And all of your truths, I forgive.

Can you hear me, Soul of mine,

Soul Divine?

I want to live. I want to live.

This consciousness is but a facet

Within your great prism

Searching for a sunbeam

To ignite my memory of you.

Lady April

The world is on the threshold of blooming

As April returns from her wandering.

Where does she go

While the soul sleeps beneath the snows,

And how does she know

When the first robin

Jewels the twilight with singing,

Ringing in pale, gold days?

Lady April, back from her wandering,

Wears a single crocus in her hair...

Incense of earth offered to the winds

And the heart, again a new canvas,

Shivers beneath the touch of sable.

Heart on the precipice of blooming,

With no knowledge of snows,

This flower has only one thought,

One thought...

And that is to bloom

For the sake of blooming.

Evolution

I bury tired dreams

As the sun shuts its eyes

Over the mountain's breast.

Though, sun, you were brief

And dreams, you were few,

You will forget me in your timeless rest,

But I will remember you.

Night folds her sapphire arms

Across the day;

I sit beneath the stars,

Wise, brokenhearted, but free.

Dreams, I watch you dance away.

Remember me.

Kindred

We were severed when the Circle began

And then severed again.

We were scattered by the winds

And thrown into Time.

We said goodbye

In the tunnel to the womb

Knowing we would always share

The same blood

And the only home we would ever find

Is in each other's eyes.

Soul Sister

Soul Brother,

I see you in the stars

And hear your voice in the sea.

You are unknown,

But I think of you

When I walk against the wind,

Knowing somewhere,

You walk a road leading into mine.

Source

We consume fruit and flesh

Of the fields;

Are we not earth?

Beneath bodily soil,

Our spirits are of the wind;

Are we not air?

Impassioned, we dance

To the heart;

We burn...Love, our fuel;

Are we not fire?

Over waves of laughter

And rocks of turmoil,

We flow urgently toward the Destination;

Are we not water?

Marlaina Donato is the author of several books including four poetry volumes and the titles *Spiritual Famine in the Age of Plenty* and *Broken Jar*. She is also a multimedia artist.

She and her beloved husband Joe live in beautiful rural New Jersey. To learn more about her books or to peruse her online visual art galleries, please visit: www.booksandbrush.net

Index to first lines

www.ingramcontent.com/pod-product-compliance
Lightning Source LLC
Chambersburg PA
CBHW070107070426
42448CB00038B/1844